Animals of the Rainforest

Debbie Croft

Contents

Rainforests

Rainforests are places where a lot of rain falls every year.
Rainforests are found in many parts of the world.
Lots of plants and animals live in rainforests.

There are four main **layers** of plants in the rainforest.

These layers are:

- the tall trees
- the smaller trees, called the **canopy**
- large plants and shrubs
- smaller plants on the rainforest floor.

Each of these layers is a home for many groups of animals.

the layers of plants in a rainforest

Animals in the Tall Trees

Eagles

Some of the largest birds in the rainforest are eagles.
They make huge nests in the tallest trees.

Eagles can see very well.
They fly in large circles high up in the sky.
Then they swoop down on their prey.
They snatch other birds, snakes and monkeys
with their strong claws.

Bats

Bats live in the tall trees of rainforests.

They sleep during the day and fly about at night to catch insects.

Bats do not flap their wings like birds.
Bats have long bones in their wings
that are covered with skin.
They move these bones so they can fly quickly
from one place to another.

Animals in the Smaller Trees

Spider Monkeys

The rainforest canopy is made up of smaller trees.

Spider monkeys hang upside down in the trees.
They use their hands, feet and tails to hold on tightly.
Sometimes, they look like spiders hanging from the branches.

These monkeys find fruits and seeds
high in the trees of the canopy.
They do not need to go onto the rainforest floor below.

Toucans

Many birds make their homes in the smaller trees.
Lots of these birds have bright feathers.

Toucans are noisy rainforest birds.
They have short, thick necks and colourful feathers.

Their large **bills** are very sharp.
They use them to **crush** fruit and berries,
and sometimes to eat small birds and lizards.

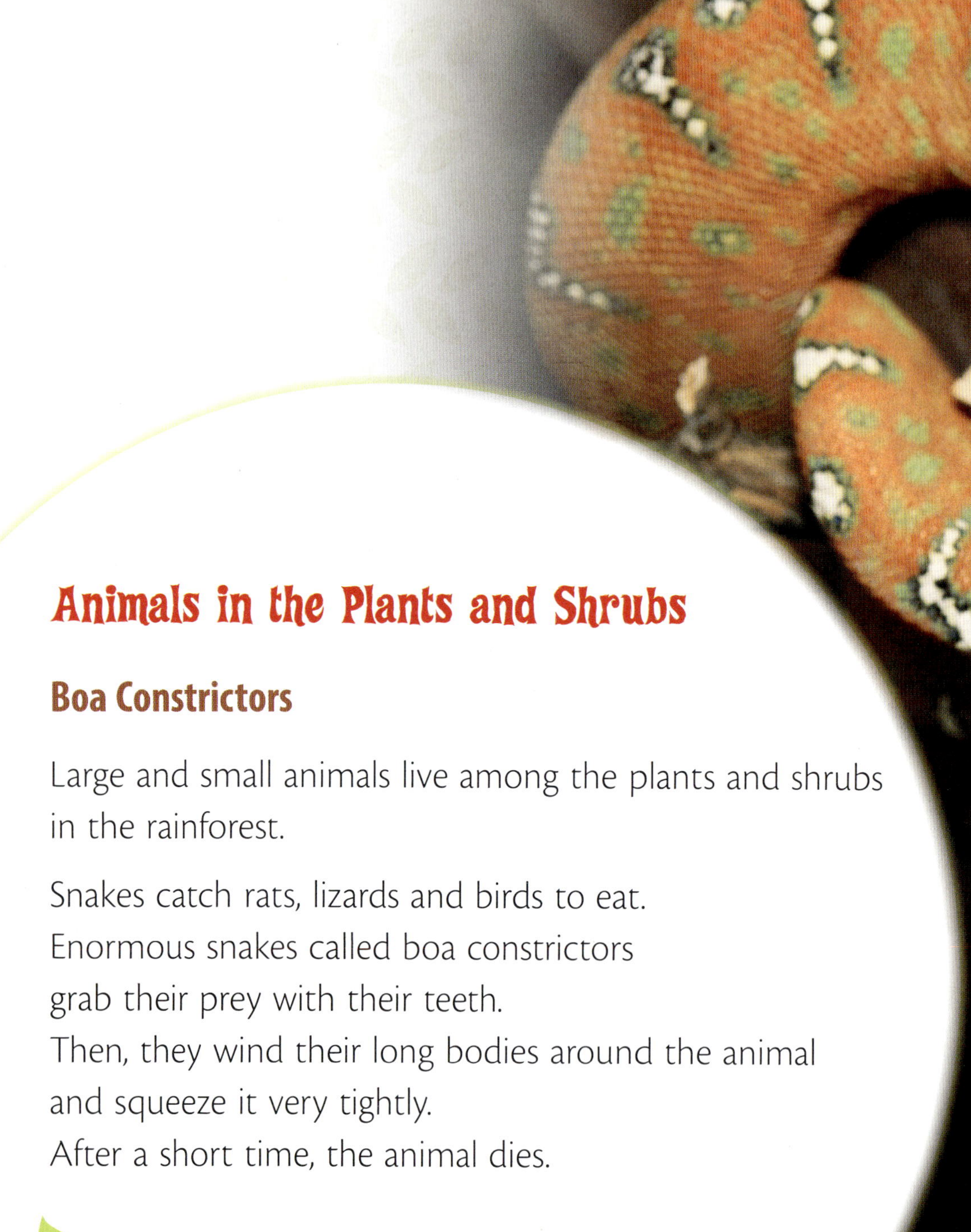

Animals in the Plants and Shrubs

Boa Constrictors

Large and small animals live among the plants and shrubs in the rainforest.

Snakes catch rats, lizards and birds to eat.
Enormous snakes called boa constrictors
grab their prey with their teeth.
Then, they wind their long bodies around the animal
and squeeze it very tightly.
After a short time, the animal dies.

Butterflies

Lots of butterflies live among the large leaves of rainforest plants.

Some butterflies have bright colours on top of their wings and large spots underneath their wings. These spots look like eyes.

When the butterflies are resting, they fold their wings together. Predators can see the "scary eyes", and this frightens them away.

This blue morpho butterfly has its wings open.

This blue morpho butterfly has its wings shut.

Animals on the Rainforest Floor

Frogs

Some tiny frogs lay their eggs on the rainforest floor.

The mother's back is covered with a sticky **slime**.
When the tadpoles hatch, they move onto their mother's back.

Then, the mother frog takes her tadpoles up into the trees, where they are safe from predators.

frog eggs

Jaguars

Jaguars are big animals that belong to the cat family.
The pads on their paws are very thick.
They can move quietly through the leaves and sticks on the rainforest floor.

Jaguars have black spots on their fur.
They cannot be seen as they hide among the bushes and trees.

Safe Homes for Rainforest Animals

Many animals that live in the wet rainforests have special ways of staying alive.

Rainforests are important places that need to be protected. They are safe homes for lots of plants and animals.

Glossary

bills *(noun)*	the beaks of birds
canopy *(noun)*	trees that make a cover for plants and shrubs
crush *(verb)*	to press or squash
layers *(noun)*	different levels
slime *(noun)*	a sticky substance